Technology in the Time of
Ancient Egypt

Judith Crosher

RSVP
**RAINTREE
STECK-VAUGHN**
P U B L I S H E R S
The Steck-Vaughn Company

Austin, Texas

Titles in the Series

Ancient Egypt   **The Aztecs**

Ancient Greece   **The Maya**

Ancient Rome   **The Vikings**

Cover picture: Using a *shaduf* to raise water
Title page: An Egyptian carpenter at work

Consultant: Dr. Richard Parkinson, British Museum

© **Copyright 1998, text, Steck-Vaughn Company**

Published by Raintree Steck-Vaughn Publishers,
an imprint of Steck-Vaughn Company

Library of Congress Cataloging-in-Publication Data
Crosher, Judith.
Technology in the time of ancient Egypt / Judith Crosher.
    p.   cm.
    Includes bibliographical references and index.
    Summary: Describes many of the innovative inventions
    that the Egyptians incorporated into their daily life,
    including ground looms, glass pots, and wooden sledges.
    ISBN 0-8172-4875-7
    1. Technology—Egypt—Juvenile literature.
    2. Egypt—Civilization—To 332 B.C.—Juvenile literature.
    [1. Technology—Egypt. 2. Egypt—Civilization—to 332 B.C.]
    I. Title.
    T27.3.E3C76   1998
    609.32—dc21   97-13922

Printed in Italy. Bound in the United States.
1 2 3 4 5 6 7 8 9 0 02 01 00 99 98

Contents

Introduction

Wherever they live, human beings need the same things: food, warmth, shelter from the weather, and a way of communicating with other people. It seems that they also need to express themselves by making beautiful things. From earliest times, humans have invented tools to help them fulfill these needs. Archaeologists define the appearance of true human beings from the time, 2.5 million years ago, when they first used tools.

The ancient Egyptians were proud of their skills. On their tomb walls, they painted craftspeople at work, weaving, carving, building, and working glass and metal. They took their most treasured possessions into their tombs, and these included their tools. This book shows you how they used these simple tools to make tiny glass beads and the great pyramids, the finest cloth in the ancient world, and paper that was used all over the Western world for hundreds of years.

Using only simple tools, the people of ancient Egypt built the magnificent pyramids.

MEDITERRANEAN SEA

Rosetta •
Alexandria •

scale
0   100 miles
0   200 km

LOWER EGYPT

Giza •
Saqqara • • Memphis

•El Amarna

RED SEA

•Thebes

UPPER EGYPT

•Aswan

Abu Simbel •

•Wadi Halfa

N

River Nile

Producing Food

All the great technological achievements of the Egyptians were made possible by farmers. In many ancient societies everyone had to spend time growing food to feed themselves. But in Egypt the soil was so fertile that farmers were able to produce enough food for the whole population. This meant that other people could become full-time craftspeople, working in their villages or in the temple or palace workshops.

Once a year, the Nile River flooded, covering the fields with a layer of rich soil. All the farmers had to do was build banks to help the water spread evenly over the fields. Their tools did not have to be complicated because the soil was soft and easy to work. Farmers usually ran what we would call a mixed farm: crops and animals. Besides their cattle, goats, pigs, and geese, they kept bees and trapped wild duck.

Plowing

This little wooden figure shows a farmer plowing. The parts of the wooden plow are tied together with rawhide—strips of animal skin that shrinks and hardens as it dries. The yoke sits on the cattle's necks and is usually tied to their horns.

Harvesting

Wooden sickles were used to harvest crops such as wheat and barley. Sharp flakes of flint, stuck in with a cement of glue and mud, were used to make the cutting edge. The reaper held the sickle in one hand, grasped a handful of wheat just below the ears with his other hand, and cut through. The stalks were left behind and were collected later to be made into baskets or used in brick making.

Catching Wild Duck

Egyptian farmers used traps to catch wild duck. Grain was sprinkled on the trap, and the farmer would then hide in the reeds. When a bird landed on the trap, the farmer pulled a string and the two sides of the trap snapped together.

Preparing Food

The most important daily job in every Egyptian kitchen was grinding wheat and barley into flour to make bread. Because bread was the basis of everyone's diet, there were more than thirty different kinds.

In Egypt's hot climate, many fresh foods spoiled quickly, which caused some problems for cooks. Meat and fish were preserved by rubbing them with salt and hanging them in the open air to dry. Then they were stored in clay pots. The milk from cows, sheep, and goats kept better if it was turned into curd cheese. Butter was made into *samn*, by heating it in a pan. As it cooled, a whitish fluid separated from the fat and sank to the bottom. The cook threw this away and kept the clear fat for frying and baking.

Most people drank beer made from fermented barley. It had to be freshly made every few days, since it went sour quickly. Wine kept well, but it was expensive, because keeping the growing grapes fully watered took a lot of work.

Making Bread

To make flour, wheat or barley was placed on a stone and crushed by rubbing it with a smaller stone. Woven rush sieves were used to remove the grit and bits of husk from the flour. In this picture, bakers are hard at work mixing, kneading, and shaping the dough. It was baked into bread in a clay oven.

Making Date Bread

The Egyptians made all kinds of bread: with or without yeast, spiced, sweetened with dates or honey, and baked in flat cakes, triangles, or clay molds shaped like flowerpots. Try this recipe for date bread—ask an adult to help you use the oven.

Preheat the oven to 350° F (180° C). Put 1²/₃ cups (250 g) of wholemeal flour into a bowl and make a hollow in the middle. Pour into the hole 1 teaspoon of oil, ²/₃ cups (about 150 ml) of warm water, and 1 teaspoon of dried yeast. Gently mix it all into a ball. Divide the ball in two and flatten each half into a round shape. Mix 3¹/₂ oz. (100 g) of dates with 1 tablespoon of honey. Spread this on one round and cover it with the other. Press the edges together. Leave it for 10 minutes to rise a little, then brush the top with honey and bake it for 15 minutes.

Making Wine

Grapes were trodden in a big tub, which had a spout for the juice to flow out, and then squeezed in a bagpress. The juice was then put in unstoppered wide-mouthed jars to ferment. When most of the sugar had turned into alcohol, the wine was strained into clay jars. Rolled rushes covered with wet clay were used as stoppers.

The Bagpress

A linen bag containing grape skins and pulp was twisted to press out any remaining juice.

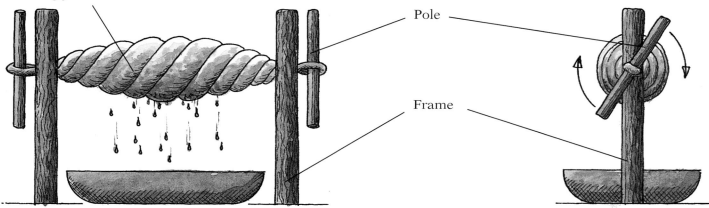

Pole

Frame

Cloth

For thousands of years, ancient peoples used plant stems to weave baskets and mats. We do not know when they first made cloth, but they must have got the idea from basket weaving. The oldest cloth found in Egypt dates from around 5000 B.C. and is made of linen, woven from the fibers of the flax plant. Flax was harvested at different stages: the younger the plant, the finer the linen. Linen was cool and hard-wearing, and it washed easily—ideal for a hot climate.

The Ground Loom

The ground loom was commonly used for weaving. This is how it worked.

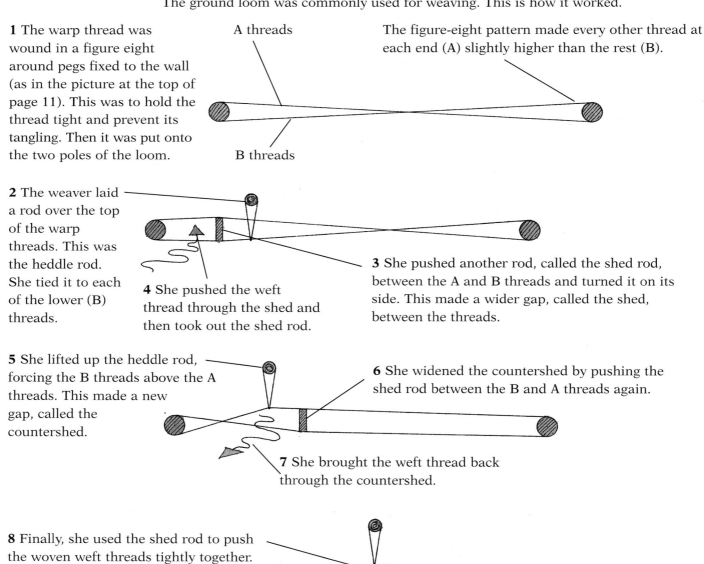

1 The warp thread was wound in a figure eight around pegs fixed to the wall (as in the picture at the top of page 11). This was to hold the thread tight and prevent its tangling. Then it was put onto the two poles of the loom.

A threads

B threads

The figure-eight pattern made every other thread at each end (A) slightly higher than the rest (B).

2 The weaver laid a rod over the top of the warp threads. This was the heddle rod. She tied it to each of the lower (B) threads.

4 She pushed the weft thread through the shed and then took out the shed rod.

3 She pushed another rod, called the shed rod, between the A and B threads and turned it on its side. This made a wider gap, called the shed, between the threads.

5 She lifted up the heddle rod, forcing the B threads above the A threads. This made a new gap, called the countershed.

6 She widened the countershed by pushing the shed rod between the B and A threads again.

7 She brought the weft thread back through the countershed.

8 Finally, she used the shed rod to push the woven weft threads tightly together. This process was repeated until the piece of cloth was complete.

Weavers at Work

In this model, the women at the front are spinning flax. On the floor behind them are clay pots containing rolls of flax fiber. With her back to the pot, each spinner pulls the fiber over her shoulder and spins it into a fine thread with her spindle. The spun thread is wound into a figure eight, using the pegs on the wall. Then it is ready to be put on the ground loom on the floor.

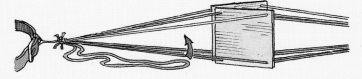

Tablet Weaving

1 Take two pieces of stiff cardboard about 4 sq. in. (10 sq. cm) and make a hole in each corner. Thread a piece of yarn about 3 ft. (1 m) long through each hole. Tie one end of the strands to something firm like a door handle.

2 Pull the other ends of the strands straight and loop them over a pencil to keep them in a line. Knot these ends together and tie them to your belt. Pull the strands tight, so the cardboard pieces lie flat with their edges toward you. There is now a gap between the upper and lower strands. This is your shed.

3 Tie another piece of yarn to your belt. Pass it through the shed from one side to the other. With a pencil, push it flat against the knot on your belt.

4 Take hold of the squares and turn them one turn away from you, so that the edges that were facing you are now at the top. This makes a new shed. Pass your weft thread back through this. Continue to turn the squares away from you, passing the weft through each time. When your braid is long enough, knot each end and trim each one to make them even.

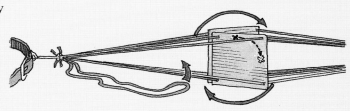

Buildings

Building Houses

In many ways, the houses of the rich and the poor were similar. They were built of the same whitewashed mud brick, although the houses of the rich had more rooms. Rich and poor used clay ovens to cook food. They slept on wooden-framed beds, which had bases made of rushes and no mattresses.

No one had running water—it had to be brought from a well in the garden or at the end of the road. However, rich families had bathrooms, and servants to pour water over them. The poor washed in a bowl in the living room. Both rich and poor used lavatory stools over a pot of sand, although the rich were able to keep their lavatory stools in a separate room.

Making Mud Bricks

Ordinary houses were built of sun-dried mud bricks.

1 Workers collected water.

2 They mixed the water with earth and a little chopped straw.

3 The mud was pressed into wooden frames and left out to dry.

Cutting Limestone Slabs

Bathrooms in richer houses were lined with thin slabs of limestone, to keep the water from dissolving the bricks. Workers used three pegs of the same length and a piece of string to make sure that the surface of each slab was perfectly flat. This simple technique was also used for the limestone slabs that formed the outer layer of the pyramids.

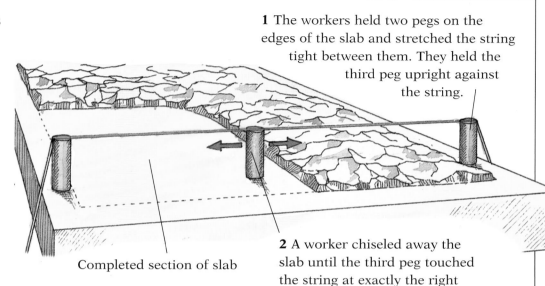

1 The workers held two pegs on the edges of the slab and stretched the string tight between them. They held the third peg upright against the string.

Completed section of slab

2 A worker chiseled away the slab until the third peg touched the string at exactly the right height.

Vent

Rainspout

Wooden supports

A Peasant Farmer's Home

On this model, there are wooden posts holding up the door and window. The roof would have been made of flat palm stems. It has a vent to catch any cooling breezes, and there is a rainspout on one side. The oven would have been in the backyard. Inside, the plaster walls might have been painted. One color scheme was a strip of black around the bottom, lines of black and red on white at a height of about 5 ft. (1.5 m), and yellow above that.

A Country House

This house was carefully designed to keep it cool and dry. It faced north, so that cool air could blow in through the *mulqufs*, the open vents on the roof. The windows high up in the walls let in air, but not direct sunlight. They had wooden shutters, but no glass. The thick mud walls were painted white to reflect the heat, and they stood on a stone base to keep the bricks from getting damp.

Water, Heat, and Light

The hot, dry climate presented the ancient Egyptians with a technological challenge: how could they make their homes cool and pleasant to live in? The answer was to design houses that kept the sun out and let the cool north wind in (see p. 13). Almost every house had a cellar for storing food. Water was stored in unglazed clay pots, like modern red flowerpots. As the water seeped through the porous walls, it evaporated, cooling the air around it. This in turn helped to keep the water inside the pots cool.

Even in Egypt, it was sometimes cold enough at night to need a fire. People who could afford it used charcoal, rather than wood, since charcoal gives a hot fire with little smoke. This was important, because the houses had no chimneys. To light their houses, the Egyptians used oil lamps. These were open clay bowls filled with oil, with a wick of twisted grass.

Making Charcoal

Wood was turned into charcoal by burning it in special pits. These were designed to keep the air out, so that the wood could not burn away completely.

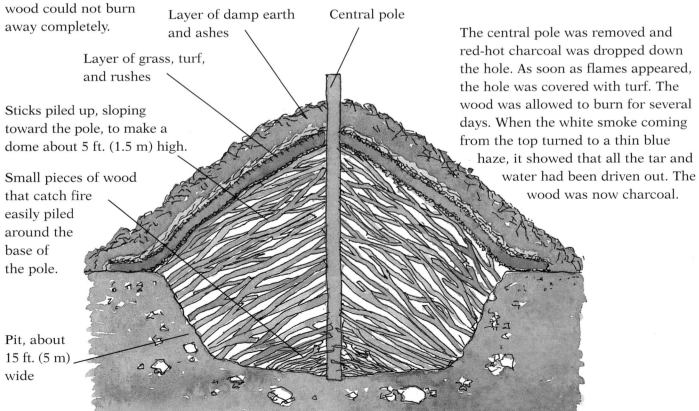

Layer of damp earth and ashes

Central pole

Layer of grass, turf, and rushes

Sticks piled up, sloping toward the pole, to make a dome about 5 ft. (1.5 m) high.

Small pieces of wood that catch fire easily piled around the base of the pole.

Pit, about 15 ft. (5 m) wide

The central pole was removed and red-hot charcoal was dropped down the hole. As soon as flames appeared, the hole was covered with turf. The wood was allowed to burn for several days. When the white smoke coming from the top turned to a thin blue haze, it showed that all the tar and water had been driven out. The wood was now charcoal.

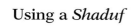

Using a *Shaduf*

The capstan handle that is used for winding a rope tied to a bucket had not been invented in the time of the ancient Egyptians. To raise water from a well, they used a *shaduf*. The pole balanced on the post. The stone on one end of the pole acted as a counterweight and helped to pull up the bucket.

Using Light to Tell Time

The Egyptians used water clocks and shadow clocks to keep track of time. You might like to try making a shadow clock. You will need three pieces of wood: two long pieces and a short piece.

1 Lay one long piece of wood on the ground and attach the short piece to one end. Attach the second long piece on top of this to form a cross-piece. In the early morning, lay the clock on an east–west line, with the head pointing east. Mark where the end of the shadow falls at 8:00 A.M. Check it again every hour until 11:00 A.M., and mark the clock each time.

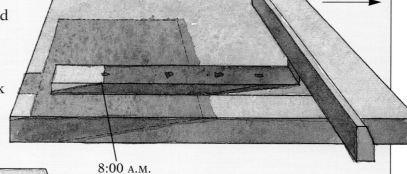

East

1:00 P.M.

West

8:00 A.M.

2 At noon, turn the clock around to face the other way. The shadow should reach the last mark (the one you made at 11:00 A.M.) at 1:00 P.M. It should mark every hour accurately until 4:00 P.M.

Working with Wood

The trees that grew in ancient Egypt—the acacia, sycamore fig, and tamarisk—were small, and their wood was full of knots. To make any large object out of wood, the Egyptians had to peg pieces together in a kind of patchwork.

When they made furniture or wooden statues, the Egyptians covered the wood by coating it with a mixture of chalk and glue, called gesso. Then they painted it or stuck on thin sheets of ivory, silver, or imported wood such as cedar or ebony. Some of the coffins that look quite solid are really made of small strips of very thin wood, glued and pegged together in layers to make what today we call plywood.

A Broken Bed

You can see how the furniture had to be built up from small pieces of wood in this broken bed end.

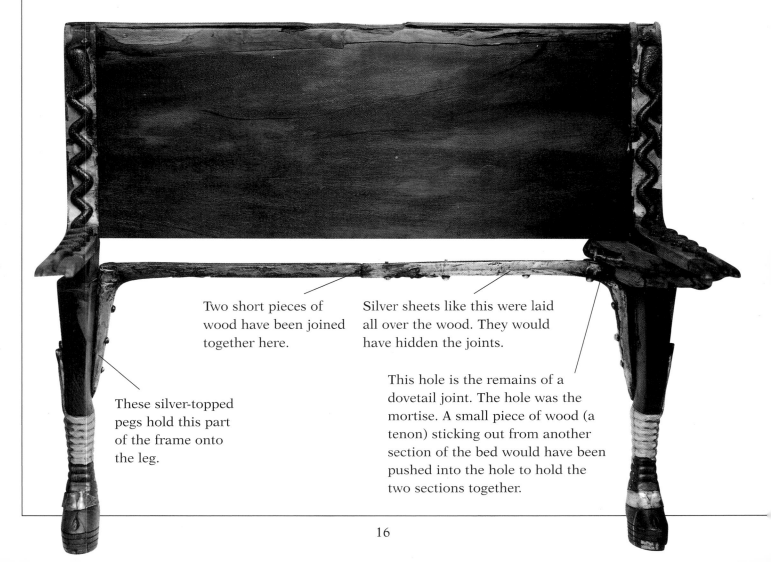

Two short pieces of wood have been joined together here.

Silver sheets like this were laid all over the wood. They would have hidden the joints.

These silver-topped pegs hold this part of the frame onto the leg.

This hole is the remains of a dovetail joint. The hole was the mortise. A small piece of wood (a tenon) sticking out from another section of the bed would have been pushed into the hole to hold the two sections together.

A Carpenter's Workshop

The teeth of the copper saw point backward. The carpenter cuts by pulling the saw toward him.

Small pieces of wood being carved by hand

Three men polishing a wooden column with a piece of sandstone. There is an adze behind them. This was used for the initial trimming and smoothing; the Egyptians did not have planes.

Two men drilling around the edge of a bed. Chisels and bradawls were also used for chipping and boring holes.

The Bow Drill

The bow drill was used by many craftspeople. You can see one being used in the picture above.

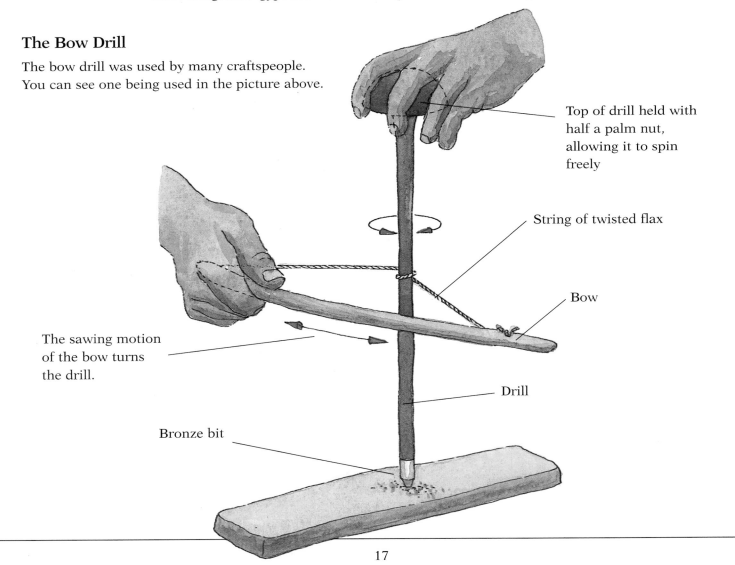

Top of drill held with half a palm nut, allowing it to spin freely

String of twisted flax

Bow

The sawing motion of the bow turns the drill.

Drill

Bronze bit

Pyramids and Temples

The great temples and pyramids are so impressive that people sometimes assume the Egyptians must have developed new technology to build them. Yet they planned and built these amazing buildings with the simple tools they had always used.

Sometimes, they used ideas they had learned in other areas of their daily lives to tackle new problems. The base of a pyramid had to be perfectly flat, but the Egyptians had no spirit levels. How could they check that the ground on which the pyramid was to stand was level? They were used to digging water channels to irrigate their fields, so now they dug narrow channels all over the rock plateau and filled them with water. Then they leveled the ground until the water in all the channels was the same depth.

Raising the Roof

The Egyptians also had to figure out how to build pillars and put roofs on their great temples. They used a similar technique to the one they used to build ceilings on their houses—but on a much bigger scale!

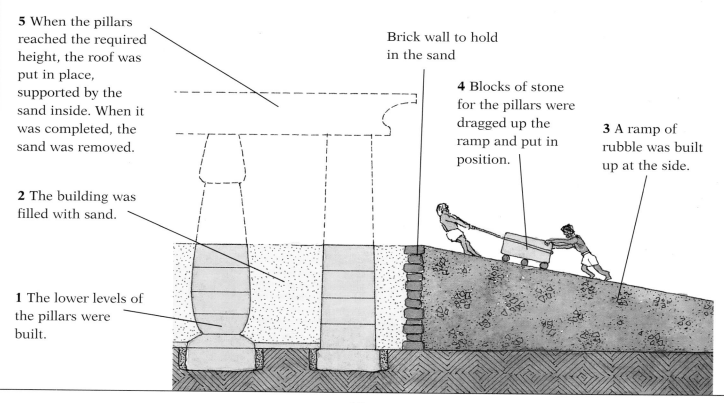

5 When the pillars reached the required height, the roof was put in place, supported by the sand inside. When it was completed, the sand was removed.

2 The building was filled with sand.

1 The lower levels of the pillars were built.

Brick wall to hold in the sand

4 Blocks of stone for the pillars were dragged up the ramp and put in position.

3 A ramp of rubble was built up at the side.

How to Find North on a Sunny Day

It was important to build a pyramid with its sides facing exactly north and south. Astronomers might have calculated this by observing the stars; another way is to use the sun.

1 Find a piece of flat ground and set up a stick in the middle. Early one sunny morning, draw a circle on the ground around the stick, making sure that the stick's shadow reaches outside your circle.

2 As the sun rises, the shadow will get shorter. When the end of the shadow just touches the line, mark this place.

3 After midday, the shadow will lengthen again. Mark the place where it just touches the line as it lengthens.

4 Draw a line on the ground between the two points you have marked. Measure this line and mark the halfway point. Now draw a line from your stick through this mark. This line points to the north.

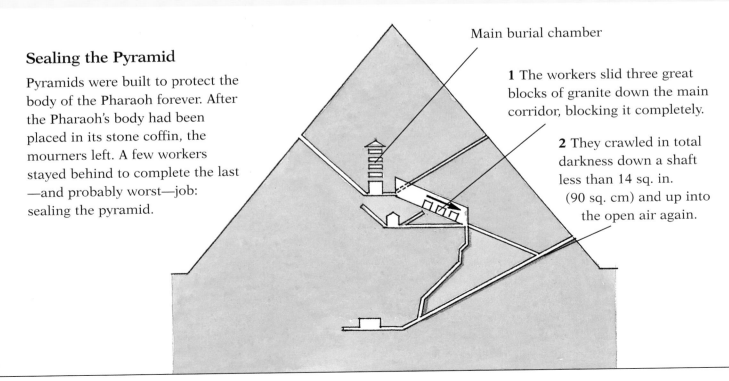

Sealing the Pyramid

Pyramids were built to protect the body of the Pharaoh forever. After the Pharaoh's body had been placed in its stone coffin, the mourners left. A few workers stayed behind to complete the last —and probably worst—job: sealing the pyramid.

Main burial chamber

1 The workers slid three great blocks of granite down the main corridor, blocking it completely.

2 They crawled in total darkness down a shaft less than 14 sq. in. (90 sq. cm) and up into the open air again.

Making Glass

The ancient Egyptians' name for glass was *aat wedhet*: "stone that flows." No one knows how the technique for making it was first discovered. We do know that by 4000 B.C. the Egyptians had learned to mix natron with sand and malachite (which produces a green color). They ground this mixture into a powder to make paint. When they brushed the powder onto a soft stone called steatite and heated it, it melted into a shiny glaze. It now looked like their favorite stone, turquoise. The Egyptians were actually making glass, but they did not think of using this glaze by itself until about 1450 B.C., when glassmakers from Syria taught them how to shape the mixture.

Glass-making took two stages. Sand and natron were heated in a little pan in a very hot, small kiln until they melted. The dirt sank and froth rose to the top. When it cooled, the dirt and froth were broken off, and colors were added to the mixture that remained. It was then put back into the kiln to melt into a thick syrup.

Making Jewelry

The Egyptians made the faience beads of this beautiful necklace from a paste of sand, natron, and water. They shaped them, baked them in a kiln, and coated them with glaze. Adding tin oxide to the glaze turned it white, cobalt made dark blue, antimony made yellow, and copper produced green.

To make round beads, Egyptians coated strong thread with paste. Without cutting through the thread, they chopped the paste into beads. The thread burned away in the kiln, leaving a hole in each bead, ready for threading into a necklace.

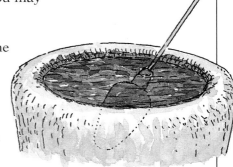

Making a Glass Pot

The Egyptians could only make small pots because they did not know how to blow glass. If you look inside a glass pot in a museum, you will see that it is rough. You may be able to see why this is so once you know how it was made.

1 The glassmaker used damp sand and dung to make the shape of the inside of the pot. He attached this core to a metal rod and baked it in a kiln until it was hard.

2 He dipped the core into a bowl of hot, melted glass, turning it to cover it evenly.

3 He dipped another rod into melted glass of a different color. He pulled out a thread of the melted glass and wound it around the pot.

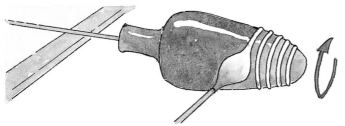

4 Using a sharp point, he dragged the colored spiral into patterns.

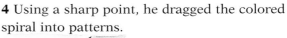

5 Then he reheated the pot to soften the glass and rolled it back and forth on a stone slab to flatten the spiral and smooth the surface. After reheating it again, he shaped the neck.

6 When the pot had cooled, he scraped out the core.

This method of decoration is called trailing. It was used in the making of this glass pot.

Metalwork

Copper and gold were the first metals that the Egyptians used, probably because they can be found as lumps of pure metal. We do not know when the Egyptians realized that copper could also be obtained by heating copper ore until the metal melted out. It was an important discovery, because there was a lot of copper ore in Egypt.

Gold is easy to work: you can join bits by hammering them together. Copper is a harder metal, and so has a wider range of uses, but pieces have to be melted together. The next crucial step in the development of metalworking was the invention of blowpipes. Several men blowing together could heat a fire enough to melt copper nuggets into a lump that could be made into really useful things, such as spears or adze blades.

A Metalworker's Workshop

About 1500 B.C., bellows were invented. The bellows was a goatskin bag tied over a shallow bowl with a tube at the front. The worker stepped on each bag in turn. Air was forced out through the tube to fan the fire.

As the worker took his foot off one bag, he pulled it up with string to fill it with air again. A valve opened at the back to draw the air in. When he stepped on the bag again, the valve closed.

Here, two men are carefully using wooden rods to lift a stone bowl full of molten bronze off the fire.

Lost-Wax Casting

The Egyptians began to use this kind of casting once they discovered that heating a little tin with the copper made a mixture that was runnier and easier to pour. This mixture, which is called bronze, is also much harder than copper alone.

1 The metalworker made a core of clay and stuck long bronze pins into it.

2 With beeswax, he molded the figure around this core.

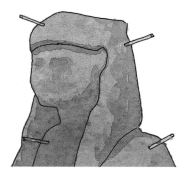

3 He covered the wax with clay.

4 It was then put into a kiln to bake the clay and melt away the wax. The pins held the core in place.

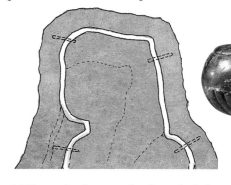

5 The metalworker poured molten bronze into the space where the wax had melted away.

6 When the bronze had cooled, he broke off the clay coat and filed off the pins.

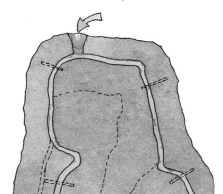

This statue of the Pharaoh Tuthmosis IV was made by the lost-wax casting process.

Pottery

An Egyptian myth tells how, after the god Khnum had created the world, he made the gods, people, and animals out of clay on his potter's wheel. Early wheels had to be spun with one hand, but a relief from about 300 B.C. shows a new kind of wheel for the first time. Khnum is shown pushing a lower turntable with his foot to spin the wheel. This kick wheel was a great improvement, because it left both the potter's hands free to work the clay. It is still used today.

Although it was probably the Egyptians who invented the kick wheel, they do not seem to have been as interested in pottery as in their other crafts. Perhaps this was because they never figured out how to glaze it with the bright, shiny colors they loved. The faience that they used for glazing beads did not stick to clay. Clay was used for useful, everyday objects: beehives, molds, jars, kitchen bowls, lamps, and cooking pots.

Potters at Work

This illustration is based on a wall painting made in 2000 B.C.

Here, a worker is preparing the kiln by lighting the fire at the base.

The potter is working with a big lump of clay on his wheel. He shapes a bowl at the top, cuts it off, and hands it to his assistant. Then he pulls up more clay from the lump to shape the next bowl.

These two men are preparing the clay by kneading it with their feet.

Here, dry pots are being loaded into the kiln for firing.

Making a Black-and-Red Pot

1 The potter shaped a large pot from red clay.

2 When the pot was almost dry, he rubbed it with a stone to smooth and polish the surface. This gave the pot a dark red shine when it had been fired and made it waterproof. Then he fired it in a kiln.

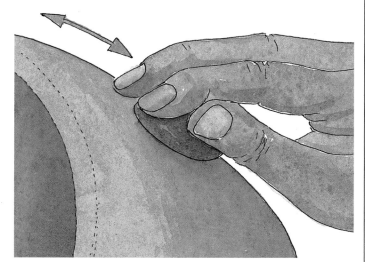

3 While the pot was still red-hot, he took it out of the kiln and stood it upside down on a layer of sawdust. To keep the sawdust around the rim of the pot from smoking and spoiling the outside, he covered it with sand. The smoldering sawdust turned the rim and inside of the pot black. To make completely black pots, he poured sawdust all over the pot.

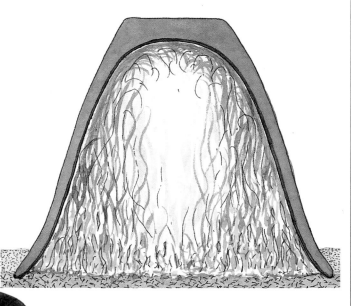

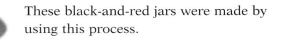

These black-and-red jars were made by using this process.

Leather, Reeds, and Rushes

The Egyptians made expert use of materials that were freely available around them. The cleaned skins of cattle, called rawhide, could be cut into strips and used to wrap joints in furniture or to bind ax blades to their handles. As the rawhide dried, it shrank and hardened, holding the joints tightly. It could be used in this way only in a hot, dry country like Egypt, because when it got wet, it stretched and eventually rotted. Rawhide could also be treated in different ways to produce leather for clothing and other purposes.

In an Egyptian home, one of the first things you would have noticed was how much furniture was made out of the rushes and reeds that grew plentifully in the marshes. The leaves and stems of these plants, together with grass and palm leaves, were used to make mats, tables, and stools, boxes for storage, and sieves for the kitchen. These items were dyed or painted in bright colors.

Making Rope

When a pyramid was being built, its base had to be exactly square. The only way of measuring it was with rope. To keep the rope from stretching, it was made with 190 strands of tightly twisted flax. Rope was also made from strips of leather. The rope maker fastened a hollow tube to a band around his waist and tied the leather strips into the tube. He spun a ball on the tube, which twisted the strips tightly together.

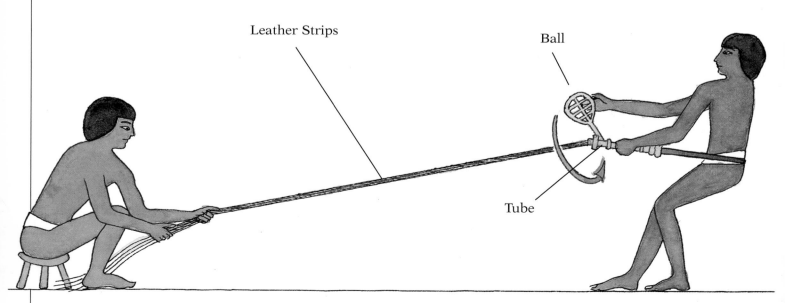

Leather Strips

Ball

Tube

Coiling

This plate (far left) is made from coils of grass bound with strips of palm leaves. Coiling is a quick and easy technique. You could try it, using straw and binding the coil with string.

Making a Reed Mat

The Egyptians made mats by weaving them on a ground loom (see p. 10) or by braiding them like this. You could try it, using pampas grass, straw, or any thick grass stem. You could even try using flattened paper drinking straws.

1 Tie three long strips of reed or straw at one end and braid them together. The trick is to make a really sharp fold in the reed each time you bend it, so it folds neatly and lies flat each time. Fasten the end of the braid. Make another braid.

2 Lay the braids side by side so the folds fit neatly together. Thread some thin string onto a long needle. Slide this through the folds all the way up. Pull the string carefully so that the braids fit together with no string showing. Add more braids to make a mat. Turn the ends over and bind them with yarn.

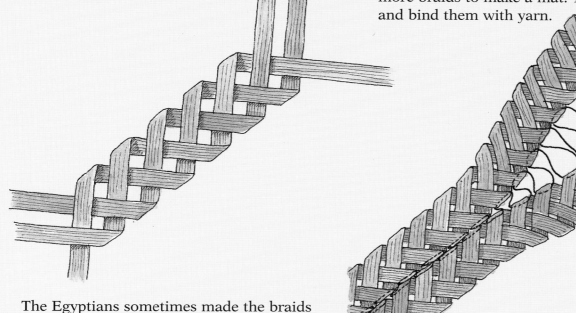

The Egyptians sometimes made the braids using five, seven, or nine strands each time.

Travel by Water

The ancient Egyptians believed that after death they would be judged by the gods. To prove that they had led good lives, they were to say, "I have given bread to the hungry, water to the thirsty, clothes to the naked, a boat to him who was boatless." This tells us how important boats were to them.

The Nile River, wide and calmly flowing from south to north, was an ideal highway through the long, narrow country. Boats came in all sizes and shapes: huge barges to carry obelisks from the stone quarries, small family boats for visiting friends, light papyrus skiffs for fishing and hunting in the marshes. A large square sail was used on boats traveling upriver, since they had the wind behind them. Long oars or paddles had to be used when traveling downriver.

Richer families had wooden boats, but poorer families could make a good small boat out of papyrus, which grew wild. Papyrus stems have thick waterproof skins around a spongy core. It was important not to break this skin, so the stems were cut when they were green and flexible.

Building a Boat

Here, boatbuilders are working on the hull of a wooden boat. They are using adzes to trim and smooth the wood.

These beams ran from side to side and from back to front to support the deck and the cargo.

A Wooden Hull

The hull had to be made from small pieces of wood jointed together. A hull like this was not very strong and could not be used for carrying very heavy loads.

The cords went through this slot and over the narrow strip of wood, holding it tightly against the joint to keep water from entering. Reeds might have been stuffed into the joint, too.

Dovetail joints held the planks together.

Moving an Obelisk

Although wood was not very suitable for building strong boats, river transport was still the best available way of moving heavy loads. This barge was made to carry two of Queen Hatshepsut's obelisks, which weighed just over 700 tons. The barge was 200 ft. (60 m) long and had to be towed by a fleet of other boats.

Obelisks

Ropes ran from bow to stern to prevent the ends of the barge from sagging.

Three rows of deck beams ran across the width of the barge to support the weight.

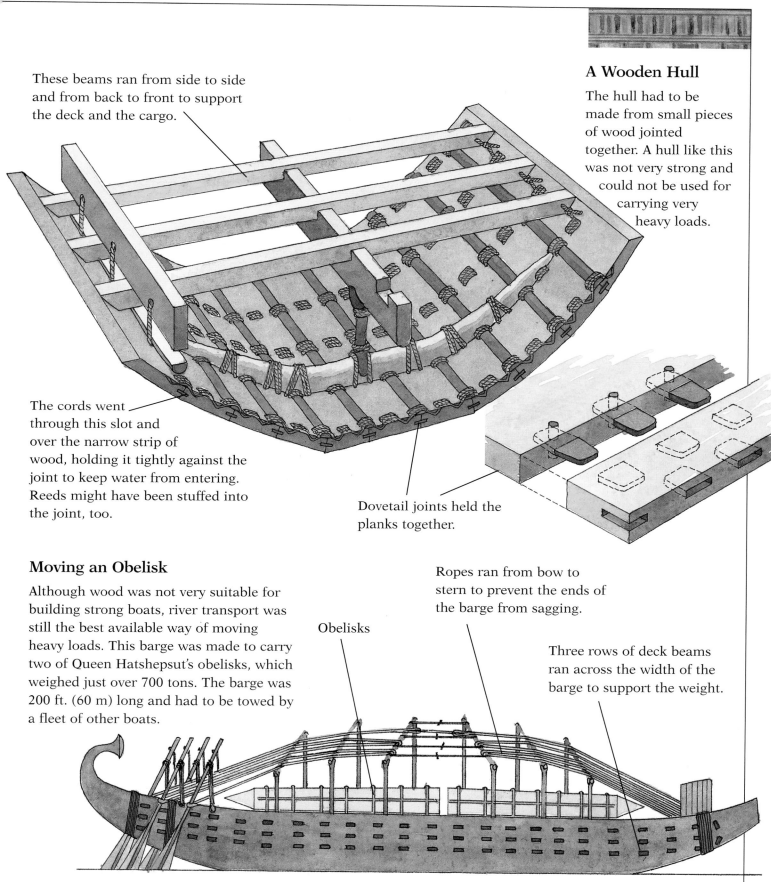

Travel by Land

The Nile River provided such a safe and convenient highway through their country that the Egyptians had no need for wheeled transport. They built towns beside the river and traveled between them by boat.

Wheels would have been no use for moving blocks of stone from the quarries to the pyramid sites—they would have sunk into the earth under the weight. The Egyptians used huge wooden sleds, dragged by teams of men, to move the stone to the river. There, it was loaded onto barges and transported to the building sites.

The Hyksos people from Asia, who invaded and ruled Egypt from about 1674 B.C., brought with them horses and war chariots. By the time the Hyksos were driven out forty years later, the Egyptians had learned how useful chariots were, not only in war, but also for hunting.

Donkey Transport

People who had to travel overland, such as farmers taking goods to market or people going to the gold mines, used donkeys to carry their goods. Here, a donkey is carrying baskets of grain.

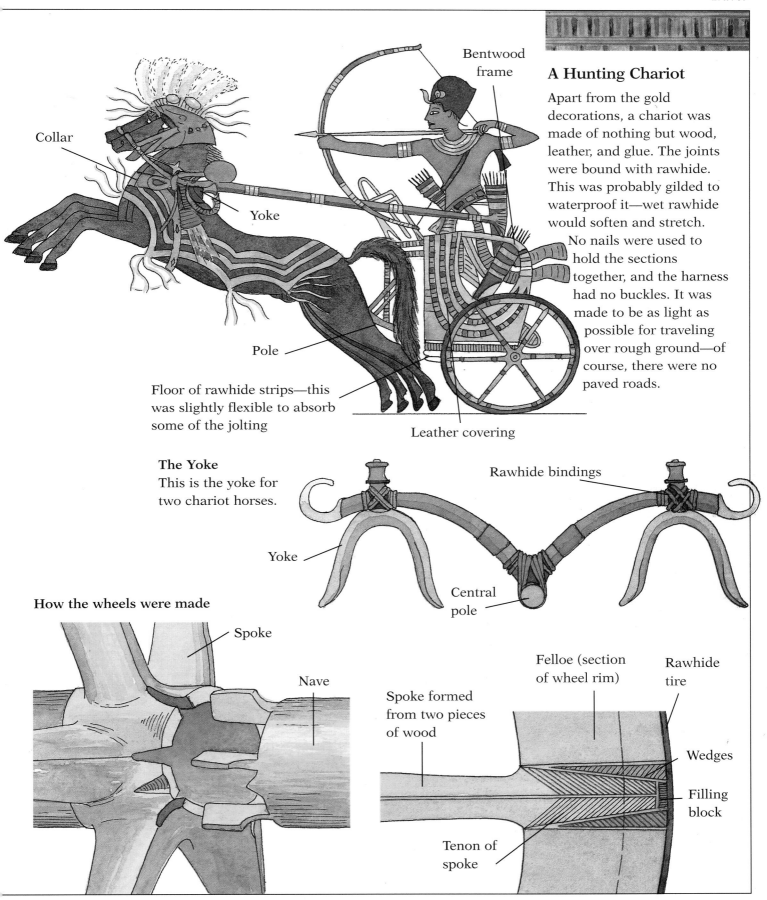

Collar

Yoke

Pole

Floor of rawhide strips—this was slightly flexible to absorb some of the jolting

Bentwood frame

Leather covering

A Hunting Chariot

Apart from the gold decorations, a chariot was made of nothing but wood, leather, and glue. The joints were bound with rawhide. This was probably gilded to waterproof it—wet rawhide would soften and stretch. No nails were used to hold the sections together, and the harness had no buckles. It was made to be as light as possible for traveling over rough ground—of course, there were no paved roads.

The Yoke

This is the yoke for two chariot horses.

Rawhide bindings

Yoke

Central pole

How the wheels were made

Spoke

Nave

Spoke formed from two pieces of wood

Felloe (section of wheel rim)

Rawhide tire

Wedges

Filling block

Tenon of spoke

33

Warfare

The technology of war has one simple aim—to make weapons that hit your enemy harder, faster, and from farther away than the ones he has. The Egyptians' weapons were axes, daggers, spears, throwing-sticks, and bows and arrows. For many years, the only important change was from using stone to using copper or bronze in the ax blades and spearheads.

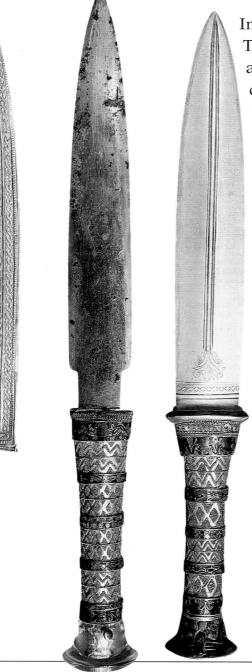

In 1674 B.C., the Hyksos people invaded from Asia. They used new weapons: horses and chariots, and a new kind of bow. By the time the Egyptians drove them out forty years later, they had learned to make and use these weapons themselves. Light, fast chariots, each with a driver and a warrior armed with a bow, spear, and shield, could do great damage to soldiers fighting on foot. The traditional Egyptian bow shot an arrow 625 ft. (190 m), but the new composite bow was much more powerful: it could send an arrow 265 ft. (80 m) farther. It was the most dangerous weapon of its time.

Weapons

These daggers and their sheaths belonged to the Pharaoh Tutankhamun. The dagger on the right is made of gold. The other dagger is made of iron and was actually more valuable, because iron was very rare in ancient Egypt. Ordinary soldiers used daggers made of copper and bronze. Metal blades were a great improvement over stone blades: it took time and skill to chip away stone to produce a blade, but anyone could sharpen a metal one.

The Composite Bow

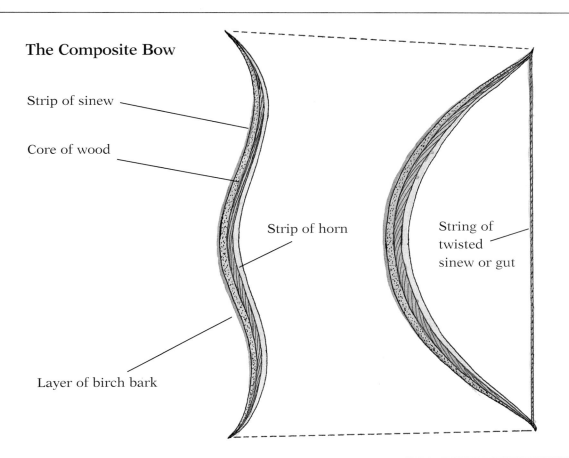

Strip of sinew

Core of wood

Strip of horn

Layer of birch bark

String of twisted sinew or gut

To string the bow, the archer pulled the ends backward, squeezing the horn layer and stretching the sinew. When he pulled the string back, the two sides were squeezed and stretched even harder, so that when he let go, the arrow was released with terrific force. The arrow itself was made of reed tipped with bronze or stone.

War Chariots

The design of war chariots and hunting chariots was the same until around 1200 B.C. The rider stood directly above the wheel and got a very rough ride, since there was no air in the tires and there were no shock absorbers. Around 1200 B.C., the wheel was moved farther back, as on the chariot in the picture.

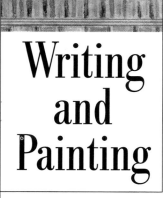

Writing and Painting

Writing

Hieroglyphs, the picture writing used by the Egyptians, were probably first invented to make lists—of kings, perhaps, or the contents of jars and sacks. The problem was that they were difficult to scribble down quickly. The busy officials called scribes, who were responsible for keeping records, soon developed a simpler set of signs called hieratic writing. They used this for everyday writing on papyrus, while hieroglyphs were used for inscriptions on tombs and monuments.

Writing Equipment

This is a scribe's palette and reed pens. The palette has two hollows, one for red paint and one for black.

Scribes at Work

These scribes are making a record of the harvest. Scribes performed many other tasks, recording food and supplies given to state workers, working in the law courts, and traveling with the army. They often had to work outside, so their writing equipment was simple and easy to carry around. Their ink was in solid cakes, like the watercolor paints we use today. By far the most commonly used color was black. It was made by scraping soot from the bottom of cooking pots, mixing it with gum, and leaving it to dry.

Making Pens

The Egyptians used the same kind of reed pen for thousands of years. You might like to try making a similar pen yourself. You can use a thin twig or long fibrous plant stem, but check first to see that it is safe to use. Crush the end and then cut it off straight. Try writing with it, using powder paint mixed with water and a little glue or lightly beaten egg white. Use the whole end to draw thick lines and the fine edge to draw thin lines. Below you can see how to write the hieroglyph that means "flax."

Twisted piece of flax

Making Papyrus Writing Paper

The Egyptians made their paper in the same way for 3,000 years.

1 Thick green papyrus stems were harvested in the marshes. At the workshop, the papermaker cut off and threw away the upper part of the stem. He stripped off the outer rind, leaving the thick, pithy core. Then, he made cuts across the top of the pith and pulled away each long, thin slice.

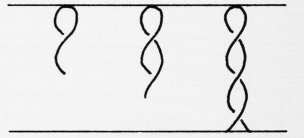

2 He laid the slices side by side on linen cloth on a stone slab and laid another layer crosswise on top. He covered them with a cloth and beat them with a flat stone for an hour or two. As the slices dried under a weight, the juice in the stems stuck the layers together to form a sheet of paper. When the papermaker had polished each sheet smooth with a stone, he joined them into a long roll with a flour-and-water glue.

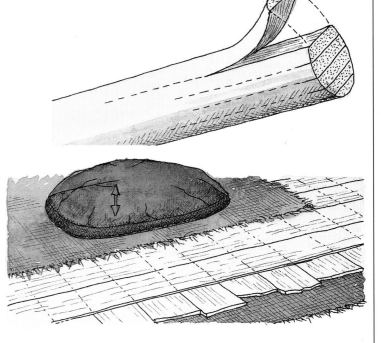

To write a letter, a scribe sat with the roll of paper held against his stomach and the end of the sheet pulled out over his knees. When he had finished writing, he cut off the sheet and rolled it up.

Painting

The Egyptians' great stone statues and the walls of their temples and palaces were once beautifully painted in bright colors, but today the paintings, exposed to air, have all worn away. The paints were made of ground stone and earth, mixed with water and gum. These dissolved in water and flaked easily.

The paintings that have survived are the ones that were never meant to be seen—those on the walls of tombs, which were sealed away from the weather. Tomb painters followed strict rules, painting the objects that the dead person would need in the afterlife. If they painted a food bowl, they had to make it clear that there was food inside it, so they showed the food balanced on top. Everyone understood that it was meant to be inside.

Drawing People

This sketch was done as the preparation for a relief on a tomb wall.

If you were asked to draw an eye on its own, you would probably draw it from the front, because you can see more of it like that. The Egyptian painters did this, too. They drew all the most recognizable parts of the body and put them together.

Planning a Painting

This is how an Egyptian painter set about his work. You might like to copy the technique.

1 The painter made lines by rubbing a string in red ocher, holding it tight at the top and bottom against a plastered wall, and twanging it sharply. You could try this, using red chalk on a large sheet of white paper fastened to the wall, or you could simply draw a grid, using a pencil and ruler.

2 On this grid, he drew the outline of the figure. However big the squares were, the proportions of the figure were always the same, for example: 3 squares from the top of the head to the end of the nose; 6 squares for the feet.

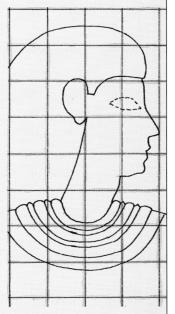

3 He filled in the outline. He did not use shading, just flat colors. Men's skin was colored a brownish red and a paler color was used for women.

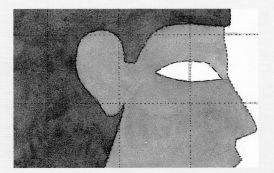

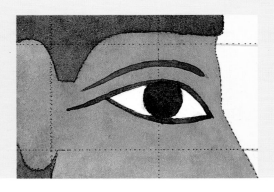

4 Finally, he put in the fine details in black and went over the outline in red.

A Realistic Image

This painting of a carpenter at work is rather unusual, because he is shown looking scruffy and unshaven. The colors used in the paints were made of ground earth and minerals. Black was made of soot, white of powdered chalk or gypsum. Reds, yellows, and browns were made of earth.

Health and Beauty

In ancient times, washing every day was quite unusual, but it was one way of keeping healthy in a hot country. The Egyptians washed with natron, which cleaned off grease and sweat. It also made their skins dry, so they rubbed themselves with oil or ox fat. The perfume industry probably developed to make these necessary oils more pleasant to use.

The dark lines the Egyptians painted around their eyes helped protect them from the glare of the sun. They used powdered black galena, which was also a mild disinfectant and gave their eyes some protection from diseases carried by flies.

Egyptian doctors were famous throughout the world and were expert surgeons. They bound together open wounds with linen strips. They made casts for broken limbs by mixing flour and cream, which set hard.

Making Perfumed Oils

The Egyptians made perfumes by soaking spices and flowers in warm oil or fat. Some of the ingredients you might be able to get in a garden or supermarket today are crushed cinnamon sticks, fresh rosemary, orange peel, mint leaves, rose petals, slices of fresh ginger, and crushed pine cones. You might also be able to get mimosa, heliotrope, or lily flowers. Try mixtures of three or four of these ingredients and choose the one you like best.

1 Pack the crushed flowers and spices to the brim of a glass jar and fill it with cooking oil. Put it on a sunny windowsill for a week, shaking it well twice a day.

2 Strain the oil. Repeat this, using the same oil and fresh ingredients for a stronger perfume.

Smelling Sweet

In this painting, the women have cones of perfumed animal fat on top of their party wigs. They probably did not really wear these —it is the artist's way of showing that they smelled strongly of perfume.

Making Wigs

All Egyptians kept their hair short, cutting it with knives; scissors were not invented until after 100 B.C. Those who could afford them wore wigs on special occasions. The wigs, like this one, were made of human hair, tied in strands onto a woven net.

Making Medicines

Through their experiments, Egyptian doctors discovered that many plants and foods could be used to treat sickness and injury. They used willow leaves to soothe inflammation. These leaves contain salicylic acid—a chemical that we still use today in the form of aspirin. They used liver, which contains vitamin A, to heal sore eyes. Copper salts, which have a drying effect, were used to dry up wounds.

41

The Afterlife

The first mummies happened naturally. Before 3200 B.C., bodies were wrapped in matting and buried in the desert. The hot, dry sand absorbed all the water from the body, preventing its decay. When rich families began to build stone-lined tombs underground, the bodies in them rotted in the damp conditions. This was a real problem, because the Egyptians believed that if the body was destroyed, so were the spirits that were supposed to live on in the afterlife. It took many experiments before they realized that to preserve the body, they had first to dry it completely.

Mummification

1 The body was washed in a solution of natron, which is slightly antiseptic.

2 The brain was removed through the nose, and the other organs, except the heart, were cut out. Then the body was laid on a sloping table, packed inside and around the outside with natron, and left to drain and dry. The organs were also dried and packed in special jars.

3 After forty days, the soggy stuffings were taken out. The body was washed, dried, and restuffed with bags of natron, sawdust, and resin. The shriveled skin was massaged with oil, and artificial eyeballs were put in the sockets. Finally, it was coated with resin and a wig was put on.

4 Now it was ready for bandaging, starting with the fingers and toes. Finally, a cartonnage mask was put on (see p. 43).

This is the mummy of Ankhef, who died around 2020 B.C. He has a cartonnage mask. Later mummies were completely covered in a cartonnage shell, and the wooden outer coffin was carved in the same shape.

Drying Flowers

The Egyptians used natron in the mummifying process. You can get an idea of how effective it was by using sodium bicarbonate. Sprinkle a thick layer on a saucer, lay a flower head on it, and cover the flower with more of the powder. Two weeks later, the flower will be dry and will have kept its color.

Making a Cartonnage Mask

Cartonnage masks were made of layers of linen and gesso. They were painted and put on a wrapped mummy, so that the person's spirits would recognize the body when they returned to the tomb.

1 Make a model of a face out of clay.

2 Cut five pieces of thin cotton cloth, or newspaper, each big enough to fit over the head.

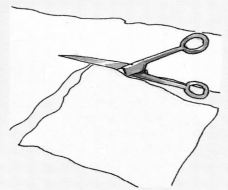

3 For the gesso, make up two cups of wallpaper paste, according to the instructions on the package, and mix in 4–5 tablespoons of plaster of Paris.

4 Dampen a piece of cloth and lay it over your model, smoothing it into creases and over bumps. Brush a thin layer of gesso all over the cloth. Let it dry a little, then add alternate layers of cloth and gesso, until you have used all the cloth. Let it dry, then brush more gesso over it to make a smooth surface to paint on.

5 When the mask is dry and hard, lift it carefully off the mold and paint it with powder paints.

Technology Through Time

The Egyptians did not keep records of when they developed a new kind of technology, so archaeologists have to work like detectives, looking for pieces of evidence and making deductions. As they make new discoveries, some of these dates may be changed.

100,000–50,000 B.C.	Tribes of wandering people appear in the Nile Valley. People dig for flint and shape it into blades and tools.
33,000 B.C.	They begin to mine for flint, digging underground tunnels 7 ft. (2 m) deep.
21,000–7000 B.C.	Wandering tribes camp beside lakes in summer, hunting animals and fishing. There is evidence of fish being dried to preserve it.
7000–5000 B.C.	People build permanent shelters around lakes and the Nile. They grow wheat and barley and make flint and stone tools. There are signs that flax is growing; tools for spinning are found.
5000–4000 B.C.	People learn to hammer small ornaments from nuggets of copper and gold. The people of Upper Egypt know how to glaze stone beads.
4000–3600 B.C.	People began to make faience jewelry. A crank drill with a stone bit is used for grinding stone vases. They extract copper from copper ore and make tools with it.
ca. 3000 B.C.	Papyrus is in use.
3600–3000 B.C.	Numerals and writing are in use. Square houses made of mud brick are built inside town walls. Pottery is decorated with figures and the first illustrations of boats.
3000–2800 B.C.	Pharaohs are buried in underground wood- or brick-lined tombs with a brick-cased hillock over them. This is the beginning of the pyramids.
ca. 2600 B.C.	Blowpipes for heating fires are in use.

These men are using blowpipes to heat a fire.

2700 B.C.	Bronze is in use.
2630 B.C.	The Step Pyramid is built, the first built in stone.
2600–2500 B.C.	Mummification is improved by removing the internal organs and drying the body in natron before bandaging it.
2416–2392 B.C.	The first illustration of a potter's wheel turned by hand dates from this time.
ca. 2000 B.C.	The use of bronze is widespread.
2000–1500 B.C.	The first medical textbook is believed to have been written. It describes surgical operations.
ca. 1880 B.C.	The first picture of an Egyptian using a foot-bellows to heat a fire to melt metal is from this time.
1700–1600 B.C.	Chariots, horses, and the composite bow are brought into Egypt.
1450–1400 B.C.	Water clocks are in use. The first glass containers were made.
1300 B.C.	The *shaduf* is introduced.
1150–1050 B.C.	The earliest surviving map dates from this time. It shows the gold mines and caves of Wadi Hammamat.
ca. 350 B.C.	A lathe for shaping wood is shown in a tomb painting from this time.
300 B.C.	The earliest picture of a kick wheel for making clay pots comes from this time.

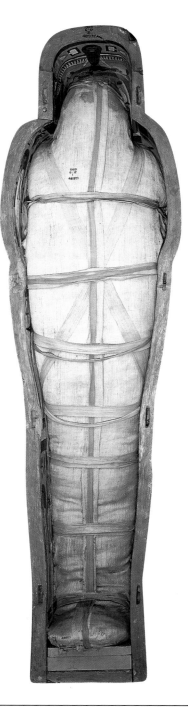

A mummy and wooden mummy case, dating from 1050 B.C.

Glossary

Adze A tool that has a blade attached to a wooden handle. It is used for smoothing wood.

Astronomy The scientific study of stars and planets.

ca. The abbreviation for the Latin word *circa*, which means "about." Historians use it when they do not know a precise date.

Faience A mixture of powdered sand, natron, and metal oxides that was used to glaze beads, tiles, and small figures.

Flax A plant, the fibers of which are used in weaving.

Flint A grayish black mineral.

Galena Lead ore (rock containing lead).

Gesso A mixture of chalk and glue that was used to fasten tiles to walls, to cover wooden statues before they were painted, and to fasten together layers of linen to make masks for mummies.

Granite A type of rock.

Malachite A bright green copper oxide.

Minerals Substances found in the ground in the form of crystals. Rocks are made up of different types of minerals.

Mortise A slot made in a piece of wood or stone.

Natron A mixture of the chemicals sodium carbonate and sodium bicarbonate. It forms naturally as a thick, dry crust around the edges of shallow lakes in the desert near Egypt.

Obelisks Stone pillars that taper toward a pyramid shape at the top.

Ocher Earth that contains iron oxide.

Ore Rock that contains metals combined with other chemicals.

Oxides Metals combined with other chemicals and found in rock.

Papyrus A large rushlike plant—up to 7 ft. (3 m) high—that grows in marshes. The same word is also used for the paper that was made from it.

Quartz A hard, glassy mineral.

Reeds Plants that grow in marshes. They have stiffer stems than rushes and are hollow.

Relief Shapes and figures carved into a flat piece of stone in such a way that they stand out from the surface.

Resin A sticky substance produced naturally by pine and fir trees. The Egyptians imported it from Syria. It was the strongest kind of glue they had.

Rushes Grassy plants that grow in marshes.

Skiffs Small, light boats.

Tenon A piece of wood or stone that sticks out from the main piece. When it is fitted into a slot (mortise) on another piece of wood or stone, it forms a joint that holds the two parts together. Also known as dovetailing.

Further Reading

Balkwill, Richard. *Food and Feasts in Ancient Egypt.* (Food and Feasts.) Parsippany, NJ: Silver Burdett Press, 1994.

Martell, Hazel Mary. *The Great Pyramid.* (Great Buildings.) Austin, TX: Raintree Steck-Vaughn, 1998.

Macaulay, David. *Pyramid.* Boston: Houghton Mifflin, 1975.

Morley, Jacqueline. *How Would You Survive as an Ancient Egyptian?* (How Would You Survive.) Danbury, CT: Franklin Watts, 1995.

Steele, Philip. *The Egyptians and the Valley of the Kings.* (Hidden Wonders.) Parsippany, NJ: Silver Burdett Press, 1994.

Picture acknowledgments

Ace 4–5/Mike Tate; AKG/Erich Lessing 9, 24, 36 (bottom); Ancient Art and Architecture Collection 13 (center), 30, 36 (top), 41 (bottom); Axiom/James H. Morris 11; British Museum 13 (bottom), 16, 25, 27, 29, 42; C. M. Dixon *cover* (background); Dr. Joann Fletcher 41 (center); Robert Harding Photo Library 7, 17, 34; Michael Holford 6, 22, 41 (top), 45; Werner Forman Archive *title page*/Staatlich Museum, Berlin, 8/Dr. E. Strouhal, 12/Dr. E. Strouhal, 21 (top)/British Museum, 23/British Museum, 32 Egyptian Museum, Turin, 35, 38/Staatlich Museum, Berlin, 39, 44; Illustrator: Tim Benké; Cover illustrator: Adam Hook

Index

Page numbers in **bold** indicate that there is information about the subject in a photograph or diagram.